COMMUNION WITH THE DEITY

A DISCOURSE UPON

COMMUNION WITH THE DEITY

Including a Memoir of the Author

By

REV. SAMUEL SHAW, M. A.

MINISTER OF THE GOSPEL

CURIOSMITH

MINNEAPOLIS

Published by Curiosmith.
Minneapolis, Minnesota.
Internet: curiosmith.com.

Previously published in Bristol: Printed by S. Farley, Castle-Green, 1765.

The text for this edition is from: *The Works of Rev. Samuel Shaw, M.A., Vol. 1.* Boston: Rev. Daniel Oliver, 1821.

Some individual words were updated.

The "Guide to the Contents" was added to this edition by the publisher.

Supplementary content, compilation, Guide to Contents, book layout and cover design:
Copyright © 2018 Charles J. Doe.

ISBN 9781946145420

GUIDE TO THE CONTENTS

GUIDE TO THE CONTENTS *(Continued)*

Memoir of
Samuel Shaw, M.A.

Mr. Samuel Shaw, M.A. was born of religious parents at Repton, in Derbyshire, in the year 1635, and educated in the free school there, at that time the best in those parts of England. He went from there to St. John's College, at Cambridge, at fourteen years of age. Here he was chamber-fellow with Dr. Morton. Upon the completion of his studies he removed to Tamworth, in Warwickshire, and was usher in the free school, and was master of the free school there in 1656. When the Rev. Mr. Blake, died in 1657, Mr. Shaw pronounced an eloquent oration at his funeral, after Mr. Anthony Burgess had preached a sermon. They both were printed, and, such as have perused them must think a conjunction of three such men as the deceased, and the two speakers, a singular happiness to that neighborhood. From Tamworth he removed to Moseley, a small place in the borders of Worcestershire, being invited there

by Colonel Greavis, of that place, who had a great
respect for Mr. Shaw, and showed him much kindness. At his coming there he was ordained by the
Classical Presbytery, at Wirksworth, in Derbyshire;
and in 1658, by the assistance of Mr. Gervas Pigot,
of Thrumpton, he obtained a presentation from the
Protector to the Rectory of Long-Whatton, worth
one hundred and fifty pounds per ann.

This was in the gift of the Crown. In June this
year, 1658, he had full and peaceable possession
of this place, and continued so to have till King
Charles's return in 1660. Upon this event, fearing
some disturbance might arise, he, in the month of
September, that year, obtained, without much difficulty, a fresh presentation under the great seal
of England, the former incumbent, Mr. Henry
Robinson, being dead, and two more who enjoyed
it after him. But though his title was thus corrobo-
rated, yet Sir John Prettyman made interest with the
Lord Chancellor Hyde, and they found means to
remove Mr. Shaw, in 1661, about a year before the
act of uniformity passed; and introduced one Mr.
Butler, who had no manner of title to the place. He
was a man of such mean qualifications, and so little
respected in the parish, that some of them told Sir
John, that they heard Mr. Butler had given him a
pair of coachmares to get for him the living; but they
would give him two pair to get him out, and put Mr.
Shaw in again. Mr. Shaw now quitted the church,

because he could not satisfy himself to conform to the new terms. Though he was not properly turned out by the uniformity act, yet he was silenced by it, and never after had any public living. He was afterwards offered his living without any other condition than that of re-ordination. But he used to say that he would not lie to God and man, in declaring his Presbyterian ordination invalid.

Upon Mr. Shaw's leaving Whatton he went to Cotes, a small village, near Loughborough, in the same county. During his residence here his family was afflicted with the plague, who received the infection from some relations that came from London to avoid it, about harvest time in 1665. He then preached in his own house to his friends and family, and afterwards published that excellent useful book, called, *The Welcome to the Plague*, from Amos 4:12. *Prepare to meet thy God, O Israel*. He buried two children, two friends, and one servant, of that dreadful distemper; but he and his wife, who both had it, escaped with their lives, not being ill both at once, and looked after, and attended one another and the rest of the family, which was a great mercy, for none of the people of the neighborhood dared come to his assistance. He was in a manner shut up for about three months together. Mr. Shaw was forced, not only to attend his sick, but to bury his dead himself in his own garden.[1]

Towards the latter end of the year, 1666, he

removed to Ashby de la Zouch, in the same county; and he was chosen to be the sole schoolmaster of the free school, in 1668. The revenue was then but small, and the school-buildings were quite out of repair, and the number of scholars few. But Mr. Shaw by his diligence, and prudent managing the business, soon got the salary augmented, not only for himself, but all succeeding schoolmasters; and by his interest among gentlemen he collected money for the building of a good school-house, and also a gallery for the convenience of the scholars in the church. Such a benefactor was he to that town, and such the lasting monuments of his praise! Then he had another difficulty, which was how to procure a license without subscription to such things as his conscience could not allow of. But this difficulty was removed, for by means of the Lord Conway, he obtained from Archbishop Sheldon a license to teach school any where in his whole province, and this without so much as once seeing or waiting upon the Archbishop. A license being also necessary from the Bishop of the Diocese, Mr. Shaw got a friend to make his application to Dr. Fuller, who was at that time Bishop of Lincoln. This friend put into his Lordship's hands Mr. Shaw's late book occasioned by the plague in his family, in order to satisfy him of the author's real worth. The Bishop was so pleased with the piety, peaceableness, humility, and learning discovered in the piece, that he gave Mr. Shaw a license on such a subscription as his own sense dictated and added, that he was glad to have so worthy a man in his Diocese upon any terms! He added, that he understood there was another book of his in print called *Immanuel*, which he desired to see.

Mr. Shaw being thus settled in his school, his piety, learning, and temper soon raised its reputation, and increased the number of scholars above any school in those parts; having often one hundred and sixty boys or more under his care; so that he always kept one, and for a great while two ushers to assist him. In this station he did excellent service in the education of youth. His own house, and others in the town, were continually full of boarders, from London and other distant parts of the kingdom. Several divines of the Church of England, namely, Mr. Sturges, of All-Saints, in Derby, Mr. Walter Horton, afterwards one of the Canons of Litchfield, and many gentlemen, physicians, lawyers, and others, owed their school-learning to his good instructions.

He endeavored to make the youth that were under his care, in love with piety, to principle them in religion betimes, by his good advice, and allure them to it by his pious example. Mr. Shaw was affable in his temper, and pleasures, and facetious in his conversation. His method of teaching was winning and easy. He had great skill in finding out the tempers and dispositions of his scholars, and adapting himself to them. He was of a peaceable disposition, very humble, and was frequently employed and very successful in his endeavors to reconcile differences among mankind. His charity was universal. He thought others were better than himself. He relieved the indigent, freely taught poor children where he discovered in them a disposition to learning, and afterwards procured them assistance to perfect their studies at the University. He did indeed excellent service in the work of education: mild and gentle in his disposition, by kindness and love he gained the hearts of his scholars. His school is said to have been of great advantage to the trading part of the town. He was of a public and generous spirit, and was always ready to encourage any good and benevolent designs. He was given to hospitality, and happy when he could make his friends so. In principle, he was moderate; but in the practice of moral virtue, he was much engaged. Though he did not, in every thing, agree with the Vicar of the place, yet he kept up a constant correspondence with him. When the liberty of the Dissenters was settled by acts of Parliament, he licensed his school for a place of religions worship, but so contrived his meetings as not to interfere with the public assemblies, nor to diminish the congregation: for he preached at noon between the sermons at church, and constantly attended there both parts of the day with all his scholars, his family and all his hearers:

so that the public assembly was hereby considerably augmented, and the weekly lecture was chiefly attended by him and his scholars. The first time he used his schoolroom he preached from Acts, 19:9. "Disputing daily in the school of one Tyrannus." But such was his prudence and conciliatory disposition, that he was on the most friendly terms with the Vicar of the place. He corresponded also with Dr. Barlow, the Bishop of Lincoln, to whom he presented his book of Meditations, which has been generally esteemed, and read with great profit. Upon which his Lordship who was a great reader and good judge of books, and as considerable a casuist as most in his age, wrote him the following letter.

My Reverend Brother,

I have received your's, and this comes (with my love and respects) to bring my thanks for the rational and pious book you so kindly sent me. Though my businesses be many, and my infirmities more, (being past 74,) yet I have read all your book, and some parts of it more than once, with great satisfaction and benefit. For in your meditations of the love of God and the world, (I am neither afraid nor unwilling to confess it, and make you my confessor) you have instructed me in several things, which I knew not before, or at least considered not so seriously, and so often as I might and ought. One great occasion or cause, why we love our gracious God less, and the world more than we should, is want of knowledge, or consideration. God himself, Isaiah 1:2, 3, complains of this, and calls heaven and earth to witness the justice of his complaints. "I have nourished and brought up children, and they have rebelled against me. The ox knoweth his owner, and the ass his master's crib, but Israel doth not know, my people doth not consider." It is strange, and yet most true, that the ox and ass, irrational and stupid creatures, should honor their masters who feed and take care of them, and yet men, rational creatures, even Israel, God's only church and people, whom he had miraculously preserved and nourished, should neither honor nor consider. This consideration is *our duty*, and the want of it *our sin*, (a sin of omission) and therefore it is no wonder if it be a moral cause or occasion of some consequent sin of commission; so that the best men, (by reason of the old man, and the remains of corruption in them) may, and many times do sin, and come short of fulfilling the law and doing their duty, when they want this consideration, or such a degree and measure of it as is required to the moral goodness of an action. Suppose a man tempted to commit adultery, murder, perjury, or any such sin; if such a man would seriously consider the nature of the sin he is going to commit, that it is a transgression of the law of his God, to whom he owes all he has, both for life and livelihood; that it pollutes his soul; that it dishonors his gracious God and heavenly Father; that it makes him obnoxious to eternal misery, both of body and soul; I say, he who considers this, as all should, would certainly be afraid to commit such impieties. Now of such considerations, you have given us many in your book, and those grounded on the clear light of nature, or on evident reason, or revelation: and it is my prayer and hope, that many may read, and (to their great benefit) remember, and practice them. I am well pleased with your discourse against usury; which, as it is commonly managed, I take to be one of the crying sins of our ungrateful nation. I remember that in 1645, in Oxford, two rich and understanding gentlemen came to the lord-primate of Ireland, Dr. Usher, desiring to know his opinion, whether usury was lawful. He knew, and they confessed, that they had money at use, and they gave their reasons which induced them to believe that their taking use was innocent and lawful. The good primate patiently heard them, and (without farther dispute, or answering their reasons, as they called them, which they had brought for the lawfulness of usury) said, "come, gentlemen, I believe you are willing in this case to take the safest way for your souls. They replied, yes, that was their desire. Well, said the primate, then your safest way will certainly be to take our blessed Saviour's advice (or command rather) and lend freely, expecting nothing,

no use again." For if you lend freely you do an act
of charity, and so are certainly secured from all fear
of sin in that particular: but if you take use, it is an
hundred to one but you sin, and become liable to
that curse and punishment which fatally follows it.
The gentlemen, like him in the Gospel, went away
sorrowful, for they were rich and had great posses-
sions, and to increase them continued their usury.
So that I think you may safely say, as you do, that
usurers are lovers of the world.

"Give me leave faithfully, and as a friend, to
add one thing more. In your second page, there is,
I believe, a little mistake. For you seem to say, that
James, who wrote the canonical epistle, was brother
to John the apostle. Now it is certain, that among
the apostles there were two of that name. 1.) James
the son of Zebedee, and brother of John. 2.) James
the son of Alpheus,[1] who was called James the less,[2]
whose mother was Mary, who was sister to the virgin
Mary; and so our blessed Saviour and James the son
of Alpheus were sisters, children, cousin-germans.
Now that James the son of Zebedee, and brother
of John, did not write that canonical epistle, will
be certain, if we consider, 1st that James, brother
of John, was slain by Herod Agrippa,[3] which was
Anno Christi 44 or 45. And 2nd, If it be considered,

1 Matthew 10:2, 3.
2 Mark 15:40.
3 Acts 12:2.

that the epistle of James was not written till the year of Christ 63. For so Baronius, Sympson, and the best chronologers assure us. They say that the epistle of James was not wrote till almost twenty years after James the brother of John was slain by Herod: and therefore it is certain he neither did nor could write it. I beg your pardon for this tedious, and I fear impertinent scribble. My love and due respects remembered. I shall pray for a blessing on you and your studies: and your prayers are heartly desired by and

>   *Your affectionate Friend and Brother,*
>   THOMAS LINCOLN.

Buckden, March, 16, 1681.

For my reverend friend, Mr. SAMUEL SHAW, at his house in Ashby de lay Zouch."

If such a correspondence as this had been carried on between the Bishops of the Church of England and Dissenters, it might have produced much better effects than the great distance which has been generally observed on both sides. So engaged was Mr. Shaw in doing good, that for the space of almost thirty years he was earnestly employed to make the world better, though with no great gains to himself. It was his chief aim to live usefully, and he thought that was considerable reward to itself. He was of middle stature, and his countenance not very penetrating; like another Melancthon, who could not fill a chair with a big look, and portly presence; but his eye was brilliant and sparkling, and his conversation witty, savory, affable and pertinent. He was ready at harmless repartees and innocent jests, with a mixture of poetry, history, and other polite learning calculated to promote cheerfulness in conversation, and was careful not to hurt the feelings of his company. But his greatest excellency lay in religious discourse, in praying, and preaching. One that knew him well has given this account of him; "I have known him spend many days and nights too in religious exercise, when the times were so dangerous that it would hazard an imprisonment for a person not to be drunk, or to be in a harlot's house, or tavern, but to be worshipping God with five or six people like-minded with himself. I have sometimes been in Mr. Shaw's company for a whole night together, when we have been obliged to steal to the place in the dark, stop out the light, and stop in the voice, by clothing and fast closing the windows, till the first day-break down a chimney has given us notice to be gone. I bless God for such seasons. If some say it was needless to do so much; I reply, the life of our souls, and eternity, which only was minded there, require more. I say, I bless God for the remembrance of them, and for Mr. Shaw at them, whose melting words in prayer I can never forget. He had a most excellent faculty in speaking to God with reverence, humility, and an holy awe of his presence, filling his mouth with arguments. By his strength he had power with God; he wept and made supplication. He found him in Bethel (such were our assemblies) and there our God spoke with us. I have heard Mr. Shaw for two or three hours together pour out prayer to God without tautology or vain repetition, with that vigor and fervor, and those holy words that imported faith and humble boldness, as have dissolved the whole company into tears, etc." In short, a mixture of so much learning and humility, wit and judgment, piety and pleasant ness, is rarely found in any, as met in Mr. Shaw. He lived beloved, and died lamented, January 22, 1696, in the fifty-ninth year of his age.

His funeral sermon was preached by Mr. William Crosse, his brother-in-law, from Luke 23:28.

> What happy prophet shall his mantle find,
> Heir to a double portion of his mind?[1]

---

1 *Epitaph to Rev. Samuel Harvey* by Dr. Isaac Watts.

ENDNOTE

1 How sore an affliction Mr. Shaw must in these circumstances have undergone cannot be easily conceived, but great, amazingly great it must have been. But hear how the good man speaks in his preface to his piece in titled, *The Welcome to the Plague*, which was drawn up and published upon the occasion. "Let me call upon men and angels, says he, to help me in celebrating the infinite and almighty grace and goodness of the eternal and blessed God, who enabled me to *abide the day of his coming*, Malachi 3:2, to stand when he appeared; and made me willing to suffer him to sit as a refiner of silver in my house—who carried me above all murmurings against, I had almost said, all remembrance of those instruments that conveyed the infection to me; who reconciled my heart to this disease, so that it seemed no more grievous or noisome than any other; who subdued me, I had almost said, brought me in love with this passage of the divine will. I can remember (alas! that I can say little more but that I do remember) how my soul was overpowered, yea, and almost ravished with the goodness, holiness, and perfection of the will of God; and verily judged it my happiness and perfection, as well as my duty to comply cheerfully with it and be molded into it; who gave me a most powerful and quick sense of the plague of a carnal heart, self-will, and inordinate creature-love, convincing me that those were infinitely worse than the plague in the flesh; who wonderfully preserved me from the assaults of the devil; never let him loose so much

as to try his strength upon my integrity, to drive me to a despondency, or to any uncharitable conclusions concerning my state; who enabled me to converse with his love and mercy in the midst of his chastening; to see his shining and smiling face through this dark cloud; yea, kept up clear and steady persuasions in my soul that I was beloved of him, though afflicted by him; who knew my soul in adversity, visited me when I was sick, and in prison, refreshed, strengthened, and comforted my inner man in a marvellous manner and measure, and made me appear to myself never less shut up, than when shut up. O would to God I might be never worse than when I was shut up of the plague! The not removing that affliction-frame I shall count a greater blessing, and a more proper mercy, than the removing that afflicted state. Who cleared up my interest in his Son, strengthened my evidence of his love, and satisfied and assured my soul of its happy state more than at all times formerly. I had clearer and surer evidences of divine grace in that patient, self-denying, self-submitting frame of spirit, than in all the duties that ever I performed. The valley of tears brought me more sight of my God, and more insight into myself, than ever the valley of vision, all duties and ordinances had done. When the Sun of righteousness arose upon my soul, and chased away all the mists and fogs of self-will, and creature-love, then also did all black and dismal fears, all gloomy doubting most sensibly flee before him. Who supplied my family from compassionate friends with all things needful for food, physic, etc. The Lord return it sevenfold into their bosom! Who maintained my health in the midst of sickness, in the midst of so great a death! I do not remember that either sorrow of mind, or sickness of body ever prevailed so much upon me, during three months seclusion, as to hinder me of my ordinary study, repast, devotions, or my necessary attendance upon my several infected rooms, and administering to the necessities of the sick. These ensuing discourses were then composed, which do at least argue that, through grace, this mind was not altogether discompsed, nor body neither. Who preserved me and gave me not up to death; for I judge that I was personally visited with the plague, though not with the sickness. Who has given me a sincere and settled resolution, and vehement desire to live entirely on, and to himself; which I account to be the only life of a soul, and only worthy to be called a living. Grant me this prayer, O most blessed and gracious God, for the sake of my only and dear Redeemer!

"Thou, O Lord God, who art witness to all my thoughts, and words, and works, knowest that in truth and soberness I publish these things to the world, not to advance the reputation of my own silly name, or to be admired of my fellow-creatures, but for the glory of thine holy name, to beget a good liking of so gracious a Creator in all thy poor creatures, who are prejudiced against thee, and thine holy service; and to strengthen the hearts of thy servants to a most firm and lasting adherence to thee, even in the greatest extremities; that thou may be admired in thy saints, and glorified for giving such power, and grace, and comfort unto men." And *O that men would praise the Lord for his goodness, and for his wonderful works to the children of men.*— PSALM 107:8.

COMMUNION WITH THE DEITY

by Rev. Samuel Shaw, M.A.

Our fellowship is with the father, and with his son Jesus Christ.—1 JOHN 1:3.

These words express the way of a Christian's living, and that kind of converse, whereby a good man is distinguished from all other men.

A good man does not differ from other men by any thing without him, any church privileges which are common to hypocrites, and sincere Christians; any external visible performances, in which the disciples of the Pharisees may be more abundant and more specious than the disciples of Christ,[1] much less by any corporeal or temporal enjoyment or ornament, strength, beauty, riches, descent, etc. nor by any natural relation, though it were to Abraham, as the Jews boasted of their father Abraham,[2] but

1 Matthew 9:14.
2 John 8:33.

by something internal, substantial, by a relation to God; the character of a good man must be fetched from his correspondence to the chief good, and the happiness of a soul must be judged of by its relation to life, and love, and blessedness itself. Things external, corporeal, temporal, make some difference among men, but it is comparatively nominal and titular: by these men are said to be rich or poor, noble or ignoble; but men are really and substantially different by the relation that they have to God; by this, they are good or bad, godly or wicked. This is the most certain and proper note of a good man, *viz.* Communion with God: in all other things he may be like other men, but in this he differs from and excels them all. This is a character proper *quarto modo;* [as logicians say] for it agrees to every good man, to none but a good man, and always to him, as we shall see hereafter. The ground of my discourse then shall be this short and plain proposition, *viz.* "A godly man has communion with God."

In order to the more distinct handling hereof, I must premise a few things briefly.

1. "That the gracious and loving God made nothing miserable of all that he made." There are no slaves born in this great house of the world. He made all things out of himself, and he has no idea of evil in himself, so that it was not possible that he should make anything evil or miserable.

Every thing was good,[1] and so in some sense happy. He was free to make the world, but making it, he could not make it evil or miserable. Every thing is the product of almighty love and goodness.

2. "The happiness of all creatures consists in their acting agreeably to that nature that God gave them, and those ends which he proposed to them, and suitably to those laws which he gave them;" which laws were contrived with the greatest suitableness to those natures, and subserviency to those ends. Every creature is in its kind happy, while its acts agreeably to that nature which the wise Creator implanted in it; as the sun runs its race without ceasing, and rejoices so to do, and is, in some sense, happy in so doing. Departing from that nature the creature becomes miserable, as the earth, bringing forth briers and thorns, instead of those good fruits which it was appointed to bring forth, is said to be cursed.[2]

3. "The happiness of the creature is higher or lower, greater or lesser, according as it comes nearer to God, or is farther off from him," according as it receives more or less from him, according to what communion it has with him. The life and happiness of the sun is much lower than that of a man, because it cannot enjoy such high and excellent communications from, or communion with God as man does.

---

1 Genesis 1:31.
2 Genesis 3:17, 18.

4. "There can be no communion without likeness." The sun shines upon a stone wall, as well as upon man, but a stone wall has no communion with the sun, because it has no eyes to see the light of it as man has, nor can receive the benign influences of its heat as the herbs do. A log of wood lies in the water as well as the fish, but it has no communion with the water, nor receives any advantage by it as the fish does. God is present, according to his infinite essence with the devils as well as with the angels, but they have no likeness in nature to him, and so no communion with him, as these have.

5. "God has given a more large and excellent capacity to man, than to any other of his creatures upon earth." God has endued man with reason, and so made him capable of a higher life, and a more excellent communion with his Maker than all the rest. The rational soul of all sublunary creatures, is alone capable to know, love, serve, enjoy, imitate God, and so to have a glorious communion with him. The sun, in all its glory and brightness, is not so excellent a being as any soul of man upon this account. And although man, by his fall, lost his actual communion with God, yet he is a reasonable creature still; he has not lost his capacity of receiving influences from him, and enjoying communion with him. The world, when it is at the darkest, is yet capable of being enlightened.

6. "When the nature of man is, by divine grace,

healed of its distempered condition, and restored to its former rectitude, to act suitably to the end for which it was made, and to spend itself upon its proper object, then man comes to have a right communion with God, and to be happy."—All rational souls are capable of holding communion with God, but all do not hold communion with him; but they that express the purity and holiness of the divine life, that know God, and live like him, these are his children,[1] and those only do rightly and really converse with him. When the Spirit of God informs these rational souls, and infuses the strength of a divine life into them, and stamps the lively impressions of divine perfections upon them, rendering our hearts, wills and ways, conformable to that glorious pattern, that infinite good, then do we enjoy a proper communion with him, and are truly blessed; though we are not completely blessed, till this conformity be perfected according to what those souls are, or may be capable of.

This is the true, and proper notion of man's communion with God, and relation to him, which we cannot fully describe, till we more fully enjoy. That soul that truly lives and feeds upon God, does enjoy more than it can tell; and yet it can tell this, that this is the most high, noble, excellent, glorious life in the world.

This communion, as also the intimateness and

1 Matthew 5:45.

closeness of it, are described variously in the Holy Scriptures, by the similitude of members being in the body,[1] of branches being in the vine,[2] by being *formed according to God's image,*[3] *changed into his image,*[4] by *God's dwelling in the soul, and the soul in him,*[5] by Christ's being formed in the soul,[6] by the soul's having Christ,[7] by Christ supping with the soul, and the soul with him.[8] Because nothing is more our own, nor more one with us, than that which we eat and drink, being incorporated into us; therefore is this spiritual communion between God and the godly soul oftentimes in Scripture described by our eating and drinking with him. Thus God was pleased to allow his people under the law, when they had offered up a part of their beasts in sacrifice to him, to sit down and feast upon the rest, as a token of that familiarity and oneness that was between him and them. By the like action our Saviour shadowed out the same mystery, when, in the sacrament of his supper, he appointed them to sit down to eat and drink with him, to intimate their feeding upon him, and most close communion

1 1 Corinthians 12:27.
2 John 15:1, 2.
3 Romans 8:29.
4 2 Corinthians 3:18.
5 1 John 4:16.
6 Galatians 4:19.
7 1 John 5:12.
8 Revelation 3:20.

with him: yea, the state of glory, which is the most perfect communion with God, is thus shadowed out.[1] And what is worth noting, I think the sacramental eating and drinking has some reference to that most intimate communion of the saints with God in glory: our Saviour himself seems to imply as much in that speech of his. *That ye may eat and drink at my table in my kingdom:*[2] in which words he seems plainly to allude to the sacramental eating and drinking which he had a little before instituted.[3] Which makes some to believe, that that gesture is to be retained in that ordinance, which is most proper and usual to express familiarity and communion; and to take away that gesture, is to destroy one great end of our Saviour in appointing this supper, which was to represent that familiar communion which is between himself and every believing soul. I will not here examine the validity of their argument, which possibly, if pressed home, might introduce a rudeness into the worship of God, under pretence of familiarity: but it seems very plain, that the nature of that ordinance does shadow out the intimate communion between God and a godly soul.

I have already, in part, prevented myself, and showed you wherein the soul's communion with God consists; but yet, to give you a more distinct

1 Matthew 8:11; Revelation 19:9.

2 Luke 22:30.

3 Luke 22:19.

knowledge of this great mystery, I shall unfold it in these three following particulars.

First, "A godly soul has communion with God in his attributes." When the soul of man is molded and formed into a resemblance of the divine nature, then has it a true fellowship with him. Now, this communion with God in his attributes is to be seen two ways.

1. "When the soul is in its measure, according to the capacity of a creature, all that which God is." This is the communion which the angels have with God; their beholding of the face of God is not to be understood of a mere speculation, or an idle gazing upon a Deity, but they see him by receiving his image upon themselves, and reflecting his glory and brightness; they partake of the goodness, purity, holiness, wisdom, righteousness of God, which makes them such glorious spirits; and the want of this makes the other, whom we call devils, to be what they are. Thus godly men shall have communion with God, they shall see God.[1] Yea, thus they have communion with him in some measure: they do not only see God in the world: as the devils do, nor see him in the Word, as many hypocritical and wicked men do, but they see him in themselves, in the frame of their own souls, they find themselves molded in his image, and a resemblance of him drawn upon them. This is a beautiful

1 Matthew 5:8; Hebrews 12:14.

vision of God, true and real, though not full and complete. This is set out in Scripture by being *holy as God is holy*,[1] *perfect as God is perfect*.[2] This our Saviour exhorts us to seek after. *Take my yoke upon you, learn of me; for I am meek and lowly*:[3] and the apostle, *Be ye followers of God, as dear children*.[4] When the nature and perfections of God, his holiness, goodness, righteousness, wisdom, etc. are copied out upon our natures, and the same spirit is in us which was in Christ Jesus, then have we a true communion with God; which blessed communion, when the soul becomes all that which God is, is by a conformity of nature.

2. "When the soul, in its actions as a creature, does rightly answer to the attributes of the Creator." As when the soul does answer the goodness of God with suitable affections of love, and joy, and delight; when the soul does correspond to the sovereignty and wisdom of God by the acts of self-denial and resignation; and does converse with the righteousness of God by patience, and a holy acquiescence. When the soul does rightly exert those acts which are proper and suitable to the nature of God, then it may be said to hold communion with him in his attributes. Now this suitableness of the soul is

---

1 1 Peter 1:16.
2 Matthew 5:48.
3 Matthew 11:29.
4 Ephesians 5:1.

especially with reference to the incommunicable attributes of God, where there is no place for imitation, though it hold good in the rest also.

Secondly, "A godly soul has communion with God in his Word." To read, profess, or hear the Word, is not to hold a real communion with God therein: many do so that are strangers to God: a man may read my letters, and yet correspond with my enemy. That son in the gospel, that heard his father's command, and answered, *I go, Sir*, but went not, had no right communion with his paternal authority. But when the soul is ennobled into such a frame as this word does require, then it holds communion with God in his Word; *e.g.* when the soul puts forth those acts of humiliation, holy fear, and reverence, godly trembling, which do suit the nature of a divine threatening, when the soul answers the command of God with suitable resolutions, repentings, reformations, and real obedience, when it entertains the promise with suitable acts of holy delight, joy, refreshment, recumbency, and acquiesces in the same, then does it truly converse with God in his Word.

Thirdly, "A godly soul has communion with God in his works." And that is, when the soul does answer the several providences of God with suitable and pertinent affections and dispositions. The godly soul does not only eye and observe the hand of God in all things that occur, but does comply with those providences, and is molded into that frame, and put upon those duties which such providences call for. Then does the soul rightly hold communion with God in his works, when it is humbled under humbling providences, is refreshed, strengthened, and grows up under prosperous providences, as they did,[1] who having rest given them, were edified, comforted, multiplied, etc. When the soul does rightly comport with every providence, and the will is molded into the will of God, then do we hold communion with him in his works. This theme is large, because the works of God are manifold, works of creation, redemption, preservation, works towards other men, and towards ourselves, both towards our outward and inward man: a godly soul has communion with God in all these; in the sense just named, though perhaps not equally in all, yet sincerely and truly.

By what has been said, you understand that right fellowship with God is not a bare communion of names. To have the name of God called upon us, and to be called Christians, or the people of God, or to name the name of God, to profess it, to cry Lord, Lord, does not make any one really and truly the better man, does not make a soul rightly happy. It is not enough to cry, *The temple of the Lord, the temple of the Lord*, with them in Jeremiah 7:4, to make our boast in the law with them,[2] to call ourselves

1 Acts 9:31.
2 Romans 2:23.

the children of Abraham, as the Jews did in John
the Baptist's time.[1] These privileges and professions
are extrinsic to the soul, and do nothing to the true
ennobling of it. But right fellowship with God is a
communion of hearts and natures, of will and affections, of interest and ends: to have one heart and
will, the same interest and ends with God, is to be
truly godly; a God-like man is the only godly man,
a Christ-like nature brought into the soul does only
denominate a man a true Christian. It is not speaking together, but loving and living together, that
brings God and the soul into one; *I live, yet not
I, but Christ that liveth in me.*[2] And thus, I suppose, you have a fair account why the apostle James,
chapter two does so much prefer works before faith,
(for indeed faith is nothing worth, save only that
faith which joins the soul to the object, and makes
the thing believed one's own) as also why the apostle
Paul prefers love before a faith of miracles.[3] Though
indeed a justifying faith is the most miraculous,
that faith that unites the soul and God together is
more excellent, and indeed more miraculous than
the faith that removes mountains. When I consider
the proper happiness, and perfection of a soul, and
the nature of this blissful communion with God,
I cannot but wonder how it is possible that men

1 Matthew 3:9.
2 Galatians 2:20.
3 1 Corinthians 13:2.

should take their communion with God to consist in a slight acquaintance with him, profession of him, and performances to him. I am confident it is not possible that men should have any true feeling of happiness in such acquaintance, any more than a man can be really filled with the seeing or carving of meat which he eats not.

Before I apply the doctrine, give me leave to lay down some rules or positions tending furthers to explain and clear it.

1. This must be held, which I touched upon before, that, "there can be no communion between God and man, but by a likeness of nature, a new; a divine principle implanted in the soul." A beast has no communion with a man, because reason, the ground of such communion, is wanting. Of all the creatures, there was none found that could be a meet help for Adam; that could be taken into the human society, till Eve was made, who was a human person. So neither can there be any conjunction of the soul with God, but by oneness of spirit. *He that is joined to the Lord is one spirit.*[1]

2. "There can be no communion with God but by a Mediator," no Mediator but Christ Jesus, who is God-man. Two cannot walk together, nor hold communion, except they be agreed: and there can be no agreement made between God and man but by Christ Jesus. Therefore it is said here, *Our*

1 1 Corinthians 6:17.

communion is with the Father and the Son, q.d.
with the Father by the Son: and faith, whereby the
soul and God are united, is still said to be *faith in
Christ*, as we find throughout the Scriptures.

3. "There can be no perfect communion with
God in this life." Our communion with heaven,
while we are upon earth, is imperfect: our resemblance to God is scant and dark in comparison of
what it shall be. We know but in part, love but in
part, enjoy but in part; we are but in part holy and
happy. There can be no perfect communion with
God, till there be a perfect reconciliation of natures
as well as persons; and that cannot be while there
is anything unlike to God in the soul, while any
impure thing dwells in the soul which cannot truly
close with God, nor God with that. The Holy Spirit
can never suffer any defiled thing to unite itself
with it; it is not lawful for "any impure thing to mix
itself with pure divinity," so Socrates the heathen.
*What communion has righteousness with unrigh-
teousness?* saith the apostle,[1] and so far as a righteous man is in any part unrighteous, so far he is a
stranger to God: the unregenerate part of a regenerate man has no more communion with God than
a wicked man, than the devil himself has, no more
than darkness has with light.

4. "Our communion with God must be
distinguished from the sense and feeling of it."

1 2 Corinthians 6:14.

Many have erred exceedingly, while they place communion with God in the sense and feeling of it, in raptures of joy, ecstacies, and transports of soul: which indeed, if they be real, are not so much it, as the flower of it, something resulting and separable from it. Communion with God cannot be lost in a saint, for then he is not a saint; for it is the peculiar characteristic of a saint to have communion with God: and a saint under desertion has communion with God even then as really, though not so feelingly, as at any other time, so far as he is sanctified. But the sense of this communion may be very much, if not altogether lost, and oftentimes is lost.

5. "A soul's communion with God cannot be interrupted by any local changes." It is a spiritual conjunction, and is not violated by any confinement; the walls of a prison cannot separate God and the godly soul; banishment cannot drive a soul from God—*Cœlum non animum mutant*, etc. [Men may change their situation, yet they cannot change the disposition, etc.] The blessed angels, those ministering spirits, when they are dispatched into the utmost ends of the world upon the service of God, are even then beholding the face of God, and enjoy as intimate communion with him as ever: the case is the same with all godly souls, whose communion with God does not depend upon any local situation; it is not thousands of miles that can beget a distance between God and the soul. Indeed nothing

but sin does it, or can do it:—*Your iniquities have separated between you and your God,*[1] nothing but sin is contrary to this divine fellowship, and so nothing but that can interrupt this spiritual society. To speak properly, sin does not so much cause the soul's distance from God, as itself is that distance. Man and wife remain one, though at a hundred miles distance; and believing souls maintain a certain spiritual communion one with another, though in several parts of the world. The society and communion of godly souls one with another, so far as it is spiritual, cannot be interrupted by bodily distance, much less than the fellowship of God with the godly man, who carries about with him, and in him, a divine nature, the image of God, a holy God-like disposition withersoever he goes.

6. "This communion with God which I have been speaking of, is much better than all outward acts and enjoyments, duties and ordinances whatsoever, though they be never so many or specious." God himself long since decided this matter, that a broken and contrite heart is better than all sacrifices,[2] that to obey was better than sacrifice,[3] that mercy was better than sacrifice,[4] that to do justly, to love mercy, and to walk humbly with God, was to be

---

1 Isaiah 59:2.
2 Psalm 51:17.
3 1 Samuel 15:22.
4 Hosea 6:6.

preferred before thousands of rams, and ten thousands of rivers of oil.[1] It holds good in reference to gospel duties, though they may seem more spiritual than the oblations of the law. A real soul-communion with God, a communion of hearts and natures, of wills and affections, of interests and ends, is infinitely more excellent than all hearing, praying, celebration of Sabbaths or sacraments,[2] as the end is more excellent than the means: for so stands the case between them.

Yea I will add, (though some proud and wanton spirits have made strange work with it, yet) it is a sure and most excellent doctrine, that this spiritual communion is a continual Sabbath, (a Sabbath of communion is much better than a Sabbath of rest) this is the Sabbath that the angels and saints in heaven keep, though they know no such thing as a first day in the week, have no reading, preaching, or praying, among them. This is a continual praying, and effectual way of praying in silence. A right, active, imbibing faith does virtually contain a prayer in it; right believing is powerful praying. The knees, eyes, and tongues, bear the least share in prayer, the whole of the work lies upon the soul, and particularly upon faith in the soul, which is indeed the life and soul of prayer. Faith can pray without words; but the most elegant words, even the phrase

1 Micah 6:7, 8.
2 James 1:25.

of angels, is not worthy to be called prayer without faith. I speak not so much of faith inditing a
prayer, or giving life to it, as of its being virtually
prayer, if not something more; for indeed faith is
a real, bringing down of that God, and sucking in
of those influences into the soul, for which prayer
only looks up for.

Communion with God is a continual fast; it
is that spiritual and most excellent way of fasting,
whereby the soul emptying itself of itself and all self-
fullness, self-sufficiency, self-confidence, receives of
God alone, and is filled therewith. A soul commun-
ing rightly with God, is a soul emptied of, and, as it
were, fasting from itself; which is the most excellent
way of fasting.

It is a continual thanksgiving; and indeed the
best way of thanksgiving in the world. To render up
ourselves to God purely and entirely, to reflect the
glory of God in an holy and god-like temper, is a
real and living thank offering. This is that hallelujah
so much spoke of, which the angels and saints in
glory do sing perpetually: what other adjunct of it
there may be, I will not here presume to say.

This communion of hearts and wills is a constant and most excellent celebration of sacraments.
The soul that is really baptized into the Spirit of the
Lord Jesus, and feeds upon God, and is one with
him, keeps a continual sacrament; without which
the sacramental eating and drinking is but an empty

and dry devotion. In a word, it is not possible for any thing that is extrinsical to the soul to make it happy; but the soul that is advanced into the noble state of communion with God, is made partaker of a new nature, and is truly happy.

Nay, further, I will add, that this communion with God is not only better than all duties and ordinances, but even better than all revelations, evidences, discoveries that can be made or given to the soul, *ab extra*, all that are from without. A manifestation of God, *i.e.* of a divine life in the soul, is much better than such a manifestation as Moses had of his glory in the cleft of the rock.[1] Many think, O if they might but be assured of the love of God, of the pardon of sin, of an interest in Christ, they should be happy! Why, I will tell you, if you had a voice from heaven, saying that you were the beloved children of God, as Christ had; an angel sent from God to tell you that you were beloved, and highly favored of God, as his mother Mary had, yet communion with God ought to be preferred before these: for these things could not make a soul happy without real communion with God, but communion with God, can and does make a soul happy without these: and to this purpose, I suppose, I may apply that famous speech of our Saviour's by way of allusion, *It is more blessed to give, than to receive*, to give up one's self, one's heart, will, interests, and affections, to God,

1 Exodus 33:22.

than to receive any external discoveries and manifestations from him. Why do we so earnestly seek after signs from without us of God's presence with us, as if there were anything better or more desirable to the soul than Emmanuel, God with us, as the apostle speaks, *Christ in us the hope of glory?* He that desires any other evidence of grace, but more grace, does not only light up a candle to see the sun by, but indeed he acts like one that thinks there is something better than God himself; though I do not say that all do think so who are covetous of such manifestations. But this I will say, and you may do well to think upon it, that holy longings after a true and spiritual communion with God do certainly spring from a divine principle in the soul; whereas a thirst after assurance of God's love, and reconciliation of our persons with him, may be only the fruit of self-love and interest. *Let me die the death of the righteous!* was the wish of a wicked man.

7. "Though communion with God concerns the whole soul, and all the faculties, affections, and motions of it," (it is God's spreading his influences, and exercising his sovereignty over all the powers of the soul, and their mutual spending of themselves upon him, and conforming to him) "yet the great acts of the soul, whereby it chiefly holds communion with God, are loving and believing." Love is the joining and knitting of the soul to God; faith is the soul's laboring after more intimate conjunction

with him, receiving influences from him, and participations of him into the soul. We may say that faith fetches in supplies from heaven, and love enjoys them; faith imbibes in sweetness and virtue from Christ, and love feeds upon it. Certainly these two eminent graces grow, live, and thrive together, and are inseparable companions. It is somewhat difficult to distinguish them, or to assign to each his proper place and work in the soul; they seem mutually to act, and to be mutually actuated by each other: perhaps the apostle might have respect to this mystery, when he speaks so doubtfully.[1] We know indeed that in the state of perfect communion, which we call glory, love shall abide and flourish more abundantly, and there shall be no room for faith there, not as to the principal act of it; but which of them has the greater part in maintaining our communion with God in this world, is not easy, nor indeed needful to determine. The godly soul is the most proper temple wherein God dwelleth, according to that, *Ye are the temple of the living God;*[2] faith and love are the *Jachin* and *Boaz*, the two great pillars which keep up the soul as a temple; take away these, and it remains a soul indeed, but the soul does not remain a temple to the Lord. In a word, these two are the soul's principal handmaids which she uses about this blessed

1 Galatians 5:6.
2 2 Corinthians 6:16.

guest; faith goes out and brings him in, and love entertains him; by faith she finds him whom she seeks, and by love she kisses him whom she finds, as the spouse is described.[1]

8. "The communion that is between God and the godly soul is altogether different from that communion that is between creatures." Here I might show you how it exceeds and excels that, in many respects; but I shall not insist upon any of those particulars, nor indeed upon any of those many differences that are between them, save only upon this one: the communion that is between creature and creature is perfect in its kind, and so, consequently, gives mutual satisfaction; I mean, it terminates the expectations, so that nothing remains to be enjoyed in them more than what is enjoyed. The creature is shallow, and soon is fathomed, we soon come to the bottom of it: a finite can grasp a finite being, and enjoy it, as I may say, all at once. A man may come so near to his friend that he can come no nearer, enjoy him as fully as he is capable of enjoying, or the other to be enjoyed: created sweetness may be exhausted to the very bottom. But the soul's communion with God does not give it any such satisfaction, though indeed, in some sense, it gives a satisfaction of a much higher and more excellent kind. I told you before, that the soul's communion with God is imperfect in this life; and therefore it

1 Song of Solomon 8:1.

must needs follow, that it cannot satisfy; that is, not terminate and fill up the desires of it. Communion with God is maintained by faith and love, as you have heard, which proves it to be very sweet; but it also admits of hope, which proves it to be not satisfactory: for where there is yet any place left for hope, there is no full or satisfactory enjoyment. This may serve as a certain mark whereby to judge of the truth of that communion with God; it is not glutting to the soul, but will certainly manifest itself in incessant hungerings, *inter opes inops*, the soul is in the midst of plenty, and yet cries out as if it were ready to starve for want. When I consider the temper of some who claim to be perfect, who decry duties and ordinances, as low and unprofitable rudiments, and boast of their full and perfect attainments, to which there can be no addition, and compare it with the temper of the great apostle, who did not reckon that he had attained, but still followed after, that he might apprehend; who forgot the things that were behind, and reached forth unto those things that were before, pressing towards the mark, etc.[1] I am ready to cry out, *Aut hic non est apostolus, aut hi non sunt apostolici;* [Either he is not an apostle, or they are not apostolic.] but an apostle he was, and had very intimate communion with his Lord: and therefore, I confess, I cannot allow these men so high a place in my

1 Philippians 3:12, 13, 14.

opinion, as they have in their own. God is infinite, and therefore though the soul may be ever grasping, yet it can never comprehend; and yet the soul finds him to be infinitely good, and so cannot cease grasping at him. The godly soul sees that there is yet much more to be enjoyed of God, and in him; and therefore, though it be very near to him, yet cries out and complains of its distance from him, O when shall I come and appear before him! Though it be united to him, yet it longs to be yet more one with him still, to be in a closer conjunction. The godly soul forgets, with Paul, what it has received, not through disingenuity or unthankfulness, but through an holy ardor and covetousness; all that he has of God seems little, because there is yet so much to be had. Though the godly soul drinks of the fountain, yet that is not enough, it would lie down by it; though it do lie down by it, yet so it is not satisfied neither, except it may bathe itself, and even be swallowed up therein. Behold a paradox! the godly soul is most thirsty, though, according to Christ's promise, it thirsts no more: it is most restless, though, according to his promise, it has rest. It is proper to God alone to rest in his love, for the creature cannot, in this imperfect state: by this we know, that we are not yet in heaven; for it is a state of perfect rest, not sloth, or cessation, but satisfaction. Faith is the fever of the soul, rendering it more thirsty, by how much the more it drinks in of the water of life; the living streams that flow from the throne of God and of the Lamb. As the waters of the sanctuary are described by the prophet, growing deeper and deeper,[1] so hope, which is the soul's appetite, grows larger and larger, and cannot be satisfied till the soul's capacity be filled up.

INFERRED COROLLARIES

Our fellowship is with the Father, and with his Son Jesus Christ.—1 JOHN 1:3.

The doctrinal part being thus briefly dispatched, it will be easy to infer some things by way of corollary.

First, "All wicked men are strangers to God." We know indeed that God, according to his infinite essence, is present with all his creatures: not only men, but even devils too, have their being in him; he has spread his omnipotence, as the foundation whereupon the whole creation does stand; he reared up the world in himself, and in him it does subsist at this day. However angels and men had sadly fallen from God, yet they may be truly said to live in him still; and although all wicked souls wander from God, as to their dispositions and affections, ingrafting themselves into another stock by sin and wickedness, yet they cannot possibly wander from

1 Ezekiel 47:3, 4, 5.

him as to their subsistence, as the apostle teaches
the Athenian Philosophers, *He is not far from every
one of us*,[1] though few feel after him or find him.
And it may be truly said, in some sense, that all
the creatures, yea, the very worst of them, have a
communion with God; all partake of him; no creature has any thing of its own really distinct from
him. Every thing that has a being has a relation to
that infinite and supreme Being; and every living
thing may be rightly said to have communion with
him who is life itself. And all those several excel-
lencies that are in the creatures are effluxes from
God, who has impressed various prints of his own
beauty and perfection upon every thing that he has
made. God's making of a thing is no other than the
communicating of himself thereunto. And therefore when you look into the world, do not view any
creature in the narrow point of its own being, but
in the unbounded essence of God, and therein love
and admire it. But upon the immortal soul of man,
God has copied out his divine perfections more
clearly and gloriously than upon any other creature
in this world. God could not make a rational soul,
without communicating his own infinite wisdom,
life, and freedom unto it: so that there is more of
the divine nature to be seen in the understanding
and will of any one man, than in the whole fabric
of heaven and earth.

1 Acts 17:27.

Notwithstanding this, wicked men are strangers to God. They live and move in God indeed, but they know it not, they consider it not, they act as if they had no dependence upon him, no relation to him. Though have some kind of communion with God, as creatures, yet this makes them not at all happy: for they are departed from God in their affections and dispositions, they have degenerated from that subserviency and subordination to the divine will, which is the proper perfection of the creature, and are *alienated from the life of God*, as the apostle speaks.[1] It is not the soul's moving *in* God, that makes it truly and happily nigh unto him, but its moving *towards* God as the chief object, and according to the will of God as the chief rule; and therefore wicked men, who pitch upon other objects, and walk by other laws, even the lusts and ordinances of their own flesh and fancy, are properly strangers to God, and miserable. He is not properly said to know God, who has a notion of him formed in his head only, but he whose heart and will is molded into a conformity to God, and to delight in him; so that a wicked man, though he know and believe, and tremble, as much as any of the devils, yet not loving nor delighting in God as his chief good, not being conformed to his image as the highest and purest perfection, may be truly said to be estranged from him; which is a state of

1 Ephesians 4:10.

hell, and death, and darkness. This is the man who, though not in words, yet interpretatively and really, says unto God, *Depart from me, I desire not the knowledge of thy ways*, with them in Job 21:14. Sinners really exempt themselves from the dominion of Christ, and do really, though not audibly, say with them in the gospel, *We will not have this man to reign over us.*[1] However men pretend, and boast of their relation to, and acquaintance with God, certainly all that live a mere sensual life, not conformed to the image of God, are truly said to be strangers to him, and in a state of non-communion with him.[2]

Secondly, "The life of a true Christian is the most high and noble life in the world"; it exceeds the life of all other men even of the greatest men. The character that is here given of the godly man is the highest that can be given of man, or indeed of any creature. It is the highest glory and excellency of the creature to partake of the life of God, of the perfections of the Creator; and such is the description that the Spirit of God here makes of the godly man. What an unreasonable and senseless reproach is that which this wicked world does cast upon religion, calling it a low and despicable thing, and upon religious and godly men, calling them low-spirited, mean people! Can a man be better spirited

1 Luke 19:14.
2 1 John 1:6; 2 Corinthians 6:14.

than when he has the Spirit of God? Can any thing more truly ennoble a soul than a divine nature? Can a man be raised any higher than to heaven itself? So noble is the godly soul, *The way of life is above to the wise;*[1] and consequently all wicked men lead a low life, and are bound under chains of death and darkness: the righteous man is of a high and divine origin, born of God, born from above; and therefore is more excellent than his neighbor, than any of his neighbors, even a king himself being judge.[2] What a wicked baseness is that sinful gallantry of spirit, what a brutishness is that sensuality of living, which the degenerate sons of Adam do so much magnify! True goodness and excellency of spirit must be measured by the proportion that it bears to the supreme good, the infinite pattern of all perfection. What excellent persons were those renowned saints of old, of whom the apostle says, that *the world was not worthy,*[3] however they were thought *not worthy to live in the world.* What a noble and generous spirit of true Christian valor, patience, meekness, contempt of the world, and self-denial, was that which was to be seen in the blessed apostles, though they were esteemed as the filth and sweepings of the world, the *off-scouring of all things?* To which of the noble, wise, mighty men

1 Proverbs 15:24.
2 Proverbs 12:26.
3 Hebrews 11:38.

of the world, as such, did God ever say, "These are the men that have fellowship with me, these are the men that lead a noble and divine life?" No, no, *not many noble are called;* and when they are called, they are made more noble than ever they were by birth or descent, by places of preferment or command. The life of every wicked man, of what rank or station soever he be in the world, is but a low life, a life in most things common to the very beasts with him. If the chief of his business and delight be to eat, and drink, and sleep, and enjoy sensual pleasures, what does he enjoy more than *the beasts that perish?* But the life of the meanest soul, that has true and spiritual communion with God, is a life common to him with the blessed angels, those *sons of the morning,* the flower of the whole creation. That life which has self for its center, must needs be a penurious and indeed a painful life: for how can the soul of man possibly feed to the full upon such spare diet, such scant fare as it finds at home? Nay, indeed how can it choose but be in pain and torture while it lays out itself upon a self-sufficiency, or creature-fullness, which is not at all commensurate to it? But the soul that rightly lays out and spends all its faculties upon the infinite and blessed God, finds all its capacities completely filled with that fountain of goodness, and itself perfectly matched with a suitable and satisfactory object. This is the true and only nobleness of spirit, when all powers and faculties of this immortal soul are exalted and advanced into a true and vital sympathy and communion with the chief Good, formed according to his will, conformed to his image.

And O that wisdom might be more *justified of her children!* O that the life of God did but clearly manifest itself, and shine forth in the lives of them that call themselves godly! Alas, that ever God himself should suffer reproach by reason of the lowspiritedness and laziness of his servants! For this cause is religion evil spoken of; the Lord awake and enable us to express and show forth the divine life with all power and vigor, to live as high as the calling wherewith we are called, and so roll away this reproach!

Thirdly, "The life of a Christian is not a heavy, sluggish thing, but active and vigorous," as the phrase, communion with God, imports. Religion is a communication of life and vigor from him who is life itself; which makes the truly god-like soul to be quick and powerful in its motions. Every thing is by so much the swifter and stronger in its motions, by how much the nearer it is to its center, as philosophy tells us. Certainly the nearer any man is to God, who is the center of souls, so much the more does he covet after more intimate communion with him, and the more eagerly lay hold upon him. Communion does necessarily imply reaction or reflection: the soul that receives of God, and his

fullness, will certainly be returning itself into him
again. Communion, in the very force of the phrase,
implies a mutuality; we cannot suppose a soul par-
taking of God, but it must needs mutually render
up itself to him again. There can be no commerce
nor correspondence without returns: but what
return can the godly soul make unto God? Why,
it renders up its whole self unto him. Faith is a giving grace as well as a receiving, it gives up the soul
back to Christ, as well as takes Christ into the soul;
it receives strength and grace from God, and reciprocally spends the same, and the whole powers of
the soul upon him. The happiness of a godly soul
does not consist in cessation and rest; the soul itself
being a powerful and active being; the happiness of
it, the very rest of it, must also be active and vigorous. Where there is communion there must needs
be quick and lively returns, reciprocations, reflec-
tions, and correspondencies; the drawings of God
are answered with the soul's running.[1] The motion
of Christ's fingers begets a motion in the Christian's
soul, *My Beloved put in his hand by the hole of the
door, and my bowels were moved for him.*[2] These
are the divine and harmonious responses which are
made and maintained in the godly soul, the temple
of the living God. O shake off that lazy and drowsy
spirit, which has so benumbed many in this cold

1 Song of Solomon 1:14.
2 Song of Solomon 5:4.

and stupid age of the world; work out your salvation with care and diligence! If your religion be nothing but a spiritual kind of sleep, your heaven will prove to be nothing but a pleasant kind of dream.

Communion with God speaks something divine, active, vigorous. The life of a Christian does not consist only in cessation from evil, reformation of sin, or dying thereunto; mortification is but one part of regeneration. It is the opinion, and, I suspect, the deceit of many nominal Christians, that if they can but keep up an indifferent, even spirit and conversation, free from gross and scandalous sins from day to day, they are happy enough; their utmost ambition is to be innocent and harmless. This indeed is necessary and praise-worthy; but surely the happiness of a soul lies higher: thus happy are all the creatures that keep in the station, and keep up the order prescribed them of God: thus happy is the sun in the firmament, running his race continually, and never departing from the office which is assigned to it. But the soul of man is capable of a higher kind of happiness, *viz.* communion with God; which is, when the faculties thereof being awakened, refined, and acted by the Spirit of God, do reciprocally act, and spend themselves upon him, longing to be perfectly swallowed up in him, and to be all that which God himself is, as far as the creature is capable of drinking in the perfections of the Creator, and become one with his Maker. This is that truly noble and divine life,

which is here called communion with God, which
the high spirited and generous soul labors yet more
and more to be growing up into, and perfected in.
Keep yourselves, with David, from your iniquities; it
is something to be freed from the guilt and power of
sin; but there is something higher than this, a more
excellent attainment, a more divine accomplish-
ment; go on therefore with the same David, and
aspire after this pure and blissful state, this heaven
upon earth, waiting for the more ample and glorious
manifestations of God to you and in you, more than
they that watch for the morning, as he did.[1] This
inference was drawn only for instruction, but the
sweetness and necessity of the subject induces me
to turn it into an earnest exhortation, from which
I would not prevent myself. Therefore I proceed to
the next way of improving this doctrine, which shall
be by way of conviction or reprehension.

1. If our fellowship *is*, that is, now exists, it
reproves them that can take up with a *shall be*, a
heaven to come. I am now speaking, not to the
worst of men, whose very souls are swallowed up in
sensual enjoyments, and imprisoned in their senses:
for these men either think of no heaven at all, or else
they place their heaven and happiness in the enjoyment of themselves or of the creature. Nor yet do I
speak to those men who, being persuaded of a future
state, do indeed wish for a heaven to come, but then

1 Psalm 130:6.

it is a poor kind of low and earthly heaven, consisting in ease, rest, safety, freedom from troubles or torments, which is the best happiness which most men understand, the highest heaven that any carnal mind can see or soar after. But I am speaking to a better and finer sort of souls than these, that verily possess a sense of a pure and spiritual heaven in the world to come; yea, they are so overpowered with the foresight of it, as earnestly expect and wish for it; yet, the hopes of it sustain and strengthen their hearts under the many temptations and persecutions of this present world; they are so verily persuaded of the truth of it, and of their own title to it too, that they are content to abide this long and disconsolate night of dimness, and anguish, and frightfulness, merely in expectation of the dawning of that day, that clear and bright day of their glorious and everlasting redemption. And in this I am far from blaming them, nay, I must needs commend their magnanimous faith and self-denial. But, in the mean time, they dwell too much upon heaven as a future state, and comfort themselves only in a happiness to come, not longing and laboring to find a heaven opened within themselves, a beginning of eternal bliss brought into themselves: they are too well contented with a certain reversion, and do not eagerly enough endeavor a present possession, to be actually instated in so much of the inheritance of souls as may fall to their share even in this lower world; this

slothful temper and inactivity I do condemn wher-
ever it is found; though it be in my own soul. Every
thing in the world, by a natural principle, thirsts
after its proper rest, and a happiness suitable to the
nature of it; no creature can be contented, though
it may be constrained, to be at a distance from its
center, but is still carried out towards its own perfection. And why then should a godly soul, who is
God's only new creature in the world, be contented
with a state of imperfection? Why should not the
saint as eagerly covet, and as earnestly pursue the
most intimate and close communion and conjunction with his God, as they do with their respective
centers? Can any earthly, sensual man be contented
with an inheritance in reversion, so as to suspend his
seeking and following of the world till some future
time? Can any ambitious spirit, who places his main
happiness and contentment in popular estimation,
and worldly greatness, be content to stand gazing at
preferments; will he be willing to sit still, and wait
till they offer themselves to him? No, no, there is
a raging thirst in the soul, which will not suffer it
to be at rest, but is still awakening and provoking
all the powers of the whole man, till they arise and
obtain water to quench it. And therefore we read
of men making haste to be rich,[1] and hastening
after another god,[2] which eager and ardent passions

---

1 Proverbs 28:22.
2 Psalm 16:4.

towards earthly objects, you may see lively described
in the Bible in the instances of Ahab, Amnon, and
Haman. And is there any reason to be given, why
that new nature and divine principle, which God
puts into regenerate souls, should not carry them
as hastily and forcibly to a present fruition of their
proper object and happiness, (so far as at present
it may be enjoyed) as that corrupt and degenerate nature does hurry them on in whom it rules,
towards the satisfaction of their base lusts? Divines
speak sometimes of making heaven and eternal life
present to themselves, and say that this is the work
of faith; which is an high and excellent doctrine,
but, I suspect, not thoroughly understood by ordinary Christians. To make heaven present to one's
self, is not only to insist upon a state of future happiness in frequent meditations, to think much of
it, neither is this that noble employment of saving
faith; but the life and power of faith is most emi-
nently exerted in imbibing participations of life and
grace from Christ, and in a real bringing down of
God and heaven into the soul. The truth is, heaven
is a state of perfect communion with God, a state
of love, joy, peace, purity, freedom; and as far as
any soul is in such a state upon earth, so far it is
above the earth, and may be said to be in heaven.
Therefore a right active soul, that truly understands
its proper and spiritual heaven and happiness, so far
as it is thus active and sensible, cannot be contented

to stay for all its happiness till the world to come; cannot be contented to be unhappy, no not for an hour, but is still growing up in God, and springing up into everlasting life.[1]

2. It reprehends them that make a stir about the kingdom of Christ in the world, and men's being brought into the communion of the church, but advance not his Kingdom in their own souls, nor long to have their own souls advanced into that noble state of communion with *the Father, and with his Son Jesus Christ.* There is, doubtless, a generation of such popular Christians, who being strangers to the life, and power, and spirit of true religion, endeavor to exhibit themselves to the world, and commend themselves to the charity of their brethren, by a pretended zeal for the kingdom of Christ in the world, and the glorious manifestation of it, as they say. I know indeed that it is worth the cares, and prayers, and utmost diligence of every serious Christian, to spread and, propagate the knowledge of the gospel, to pour out the ointment of Christ's name far and near. A more pure and spiritual administration of all gospel ordinances throughout the world is highly desirable; yea, and I think an indifferent and careless disposition towards the worship of God, argues much of an earthly and atheistical mind. But I fear, that the kingdom of Christ, and those glorious manifestations and discoveries which are

1 John 4:14.

so much pretended to by many, if they should be thoroughly examined, would be, at length, resolved into nothing else but the advancement of some one party or interest above all the rest, or the exchanging of an old form and dress of religion for a new one; and that this zeal would be found little better than the blazings of self love, a fire kindled not by a coal from the altar, but by a spark of their own. But, be it so, that this disposition of theirs is sincere and spiritual; should not their charity begin at home? The most proper kingdom of Christ is that whereby he rules in the hearts of men; the most excellent worship is when the soul itself becomes a temple for the living God to dwell in, and to receive and reflect the manifestations of his glory, when a fire of divine love is kindled in it, and therein it does offer up, not bulls and goats, no, nor so much prayers and meditations, as indeed itself unto God, which is a reasonable service, as the apostle speaks, far more glorious than either the Mosaical or Evangelical dispensation, if you consider it in the letter only. Whatever men may pretend, no man can be truly and rightly studious of the advancement of the kingdom of God in the world, that has not first felt the mighty power, and blessed effects of it in his own soul. Communion with the church is only so far to be valued, as it lies in order to a real and spiritual communion with God; which communion with God, if we do indeed sincerely wish to others, we shall more abundantly labor to promote in ourselves. I cannot believe that he does heartily seek the happiness of others, who himself sits still, and is content to be miserable, especially when their happiness and his is one and the same.

3. It condemns them as not Christians, whose fellowship is only with their fellow creatures. We have seen that this is the character, the distinguishing character of a godly man, to have fellowship with God; it must needs follow then, that those degenerate souls that rise no higher than the world, that converse only with self or any other creature, are verily strangers to true Christianity, whatever their confidence or presumption may be. Christians, tell me not what you profess of Christ, what you believe of the gospel, what orthodox opinions you hold, what an honest party you side with, how many and specious duties you perform, no, nor what hopes or wishes you have of going to heaven; but tell me where is your principal communion; what do you principally mind, follow, converse with; to what pattern do you conform; by which rule do you live; what object do you ultimately aim at? The whole world of ungodly men does hasten after another god, as the Psalmist's phrase is, though not all after the same god; they spend their souls indeed upon various objects, and use different methods to obtain rest; but yet all their happiness and contentment are ultimately resolved into creature communion.

That dreadful sentence, that the apostle delivers universally concerning all men, is to be limited to all wicked men only, and of them it is undoubtedly true, *All seek their own, and none the things of Jesus Christ:*[1] and of all these the Psalmist's *many* is to be understood, *There be many that say, Who will show us any good?*[2] *i.e.* any creature-good, as the words following do explain it. All unregenerate souls are bound up in the creature, some creature or other; and therefore the noblest of them, whatever boasts they may make, are low and ignoble; their main converse is but with their fellow creatures, and indeed creatures much inferior to themselves, *corn and wine*, says the Psalmist, *earthly things*, says the apostle, *Who mind earthly things.*[3] In a word, though it be true what the apostle says in one place, that all men in the world do live in God,[4] yet it is also true, that most men, as the same apostle speaks elsewhere, do live *without God in the world*, have their hearts fastened down to one creature or other, and so fall short of this honorable character which the apostle here gives of godly men; *Our fellowship is with the Father, and with his Son Jesus Christ.*

I shall close the remainder of this discourse,

---

1 Philippians 2:21.
2 Psalm 4:6.
3 Philippians 3:19.
4 Acts 17:28.

with an humble request and earnest expostulation.

"Reckon not upon any happiness short of this communion." There are many things which a Christian may take to be comforts; but only one, this one, that he ought to take to be the happiness of his life. I design not to speak any thing to the prejudice of natural or civil ornaments or accomplishments, much less to the disparagement of any of those endowments or employments, which are, in a sense, spiritual, commonly called gifts and duties; but I confess, I wonder that such a noble and intelligent being as the soul of man should attend to, and pursue after things either extrinsical or inferior to itself, and in the mean time carelessly forget, or wilfully reject its main happiness, principal end, and proper perfection. As for those sensual persons, those mere animals, whose souls are incarnate in their senses, and seem to perform no higher office in the world than the souls of beasts, that is, to carry about their bodies, who value themselves by their bodies, or which is baser, by the apparel that clothes them, or the estates that feed them, I shall not now trouble myself about them, but leave them to be chastised by Seneca or Plutarch, or indeed any ordinary philosopher.

I shall rather apply myself a little to a sort of higher spirited people, whom by a condescension of charity, we call Christians, who, valuing themselves by external professions, privileges, performances, may indeed be said to be somewhat more scrupulous and curious, but no less mistaken than the former: for if the grosser sort of sensualists deny and professedly abjure their own reason, and the finer sort of hypocrites more cunningly bribe theirs, each method amounts to no more than a cheat, and both parties, will be alike miserable, only the latter will be somewhat more tormented in missing of a happiness which he looked and hoped for. It is not suit my present discourse, to speak so highly and honorably of these externals of Christianity, nor to press them so zealously, as I do at all times when I have occasion; for I do verily value all ordinances of Christ, and duties of God's worship at a high rate; nay, I know not any serious and truly godly soul in the world, who is not of the same profession with me; but I must confess, I think it is one of the greatest and most pernicious cheats in the world, for men to feed upon the dish instead of the meat, to place their happiness in those things which God has only appointed to be means to convey it.

This was the great destruction of the Jewish church; by this they perished: thus they are every where described in Scripture, as a people resting in their privileges and performances, boasting of their sacrifices and temple service; they expected a strange kind of flesh-pleasing heaven something distinct from them, and reserved for them, to be given them by way of reward for the righteousness which they themselves had wrought by the power of their own free will (which free will, they say is an effect of man's fall, but they make it a cause of man's rise; for now he can purchase and merit a happiness, which happiness is also more illustrious than that given of mere grace) which righteousness, if we look either into their own writings, or God's writings concerning them, we shall find was nothing else but a strict observance of the precepts of the law, according to the letter and external dispensation of it. Such a low and legal spirit was generally found among the Jews; I wish the greatest part of us, who are in profession and name evangelical, may not be found as truly legal in spirit and temper as they were. If we cry, The Gospel of Christ, the Gospel of Christ; with the same spirit as they cried, *The temple of the Lord, the temple of the Lord;* our confidence will as surely betray us into a final misery as theirs did. True, indeed, prayers, sacraments, sermons, are somewhat finer words than the old obsolete ones, the law, sacrifices, ceremonies; but, alas! they are but words; at least they are not gods, of course, no more fit to terminate our devotions and affections than these. I beseech you, therefore, Christians, be not mistaken in this matter. True Christianity is not a notion but a nature; that is not religion which is treasured up in books, or laid up in men's understandings, but it is laid in the very constitution of the soul, it is a new principle implanted by

God in the highest powers of the soul, refining and spiritualizing all the faculties thereof, and rendering them as like to God himself, as such a creature can resemble its Creator.

It is a truth as clear as the sun, that nothing can make a soul truly happy but what is wrought into the nature of it, which must be something more excellent than itself, and can be nothing less than something divine, even the image of the blessed God. If you be Christians in deed and in truth, value all the ordinances of God, and the duties of the Christian religion, but value not yourselves or your happiness by these; attend upon them all for the maintaining and increasing of real fellowship with God; for though these be not it, yet they are the way wherein it pleases God to give it; drink the sincere milk of the Word, but let it be only with a holy design of growing thereby, of growing up into God, and a divine life. Away with those low and base thoughts of happiness; the happiness of a soul is a high and excellent, indeed a divine thing; it is in some sense common to God and the soul; God is happy in himself alone, and the soul can only be happy in him. What contentment, what real happiness, Christian, can the rising of your party in the world, or the rising of your name in the country bring thee, if, in the mean time, you yourself harbor any carnal will or self-interest that does rise up in opposition to the pure and perfect will and nature of God? How are you happy in your prayers, if you cast sin out at your mouth, and in the mean time a fountain of iniquity be springing up in your heart? What avails it towards a state of perfection to be of the most orthodox opinions, the honorable society, the fairest profession, the most popular and sanctimonious form, or the most plausible performances, if the soul is in the mean time alienated from the life of God, and feeds upon some earthly trash or other, which destroys the native powers and vigor of it, and keeps it under a perpetual languor? As much as a silken stocking on a broken leg, or a princely diadem upon an aching head, avails towards a state of ease and soundness of body. Let nothing limit your ambition but a state of god-like perfection; let nothing set bounds to your loving and longing souls, but a real fruition of God himself: nay, let not that bound them neither, but the more you enjoy, see, and taste, the more let your love be strengthened; after the manner of fire, which, the more it is fed, the more hungry and devouring it grows. In a word, let nothing satisfy you but the highest character that can be given of mortal men, to be men *after God's own heart*, to have God dwelling in you, to be filled with his fullness, to have this real and excellent *communion with the Father, and with his Son Jesus Christ*. To whom be all honor, praise, and glory, for ever and ever!—*Amen*.

www.ingramcontent.com/pod-product-compliance
Lightning Source LLC
Chambersburg PA
CBHW020604030426
42337CB00013B/1212